998
WAT
C.1
2002
12.95

3
OFF

2
WR

1
QB

1
RB

DATE DUE

205

C.1                           2002

2-3
DIFF

2
CB

1
S

1
LB

Offensive
Offense

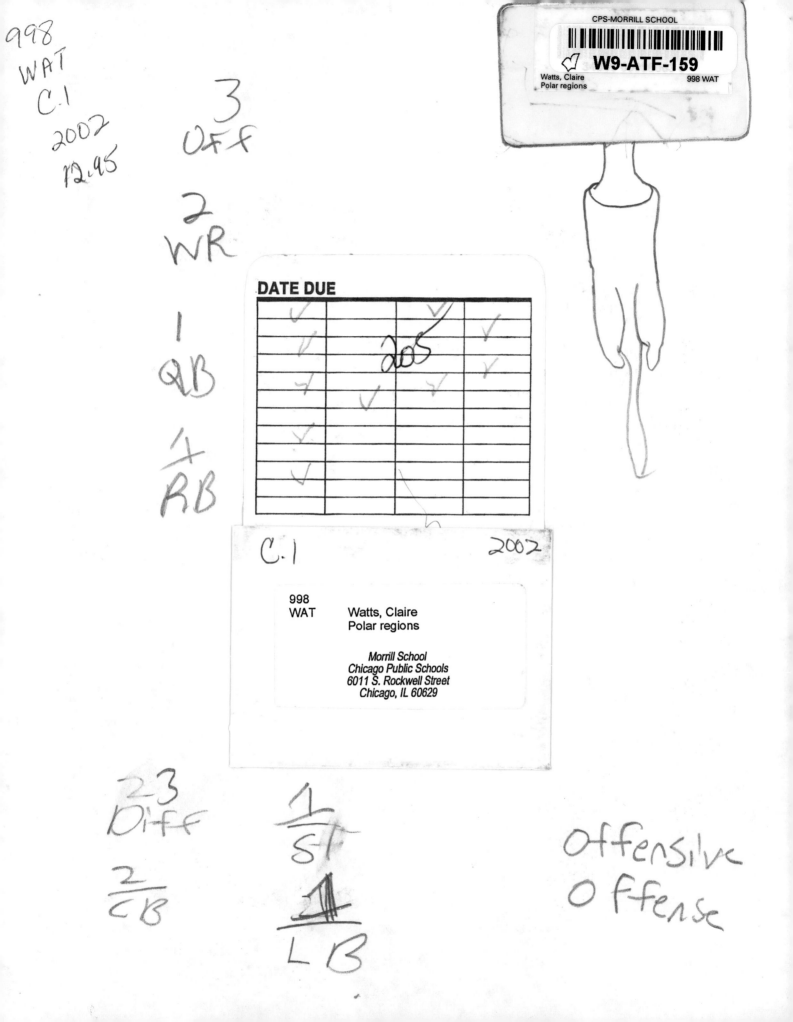

LAUNCH PAD
LIBRARY

12.95
2002

# POLAR
# REGIONS

### CLAIRE WATTS

STAMPLEY

# How to Use This Book

## Cross-references
Above some of the chapter titles, you will find a list of other chapters in the book that are related to the topic. Turn to these pages to find out more about each subject.

## See for yourself
See-for-yourself bubbles give you the chance to test out some of the ideas in this book. They explain what you will need and what you have to do to see if an idea really works.

## Quiz corner
In the quiz corner, you will find a list of questions. The answers to the quiz questions are somewhere in the same chapter. Try to answer all the questions about each subject.

## Chatterboxes
Chatterboxes give you interesting facts about other things that are related to the subject.

## Glossary
Difficult words are explained in the glossary on page 31. These words are in **bold** type in the book. Look them up in the glossary to find out what they mean.

## Index
The index is on page 32. It is a list of important words mentioned in the book, with page numbers next to the entries. If you want to read about a subject, look it up in the index, then turn to the page number given.

# Contents

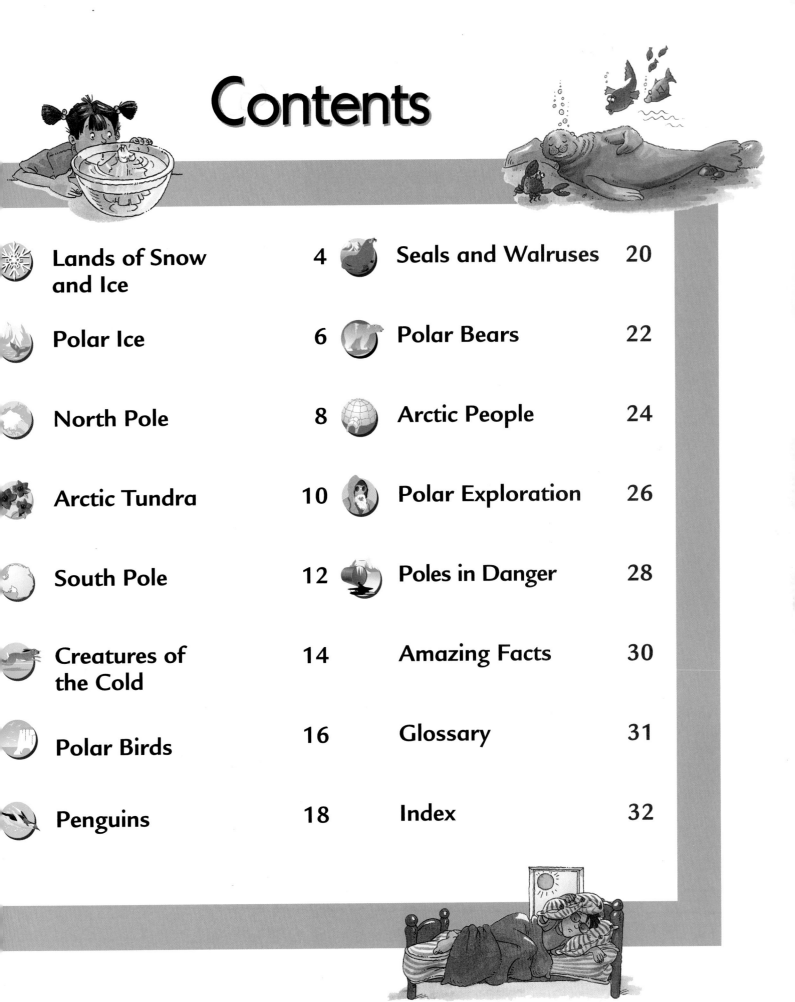

# Lands of Snow and Ice

The polar lands are among the coldest places on Earth. Many parts are covered in snow or ice all year round. On a globe or a map of the world, the South Pole is at the bottom and the North Pole is at the top.

**Why are the Poles cold?**
Around the middle of the Earth, the sun's rays fall close together, making the lands there hot. At the Poles, the Earth curves away from the sun, so the rays spread over a wider area. This weakens the sun's power, making the Poles cold.

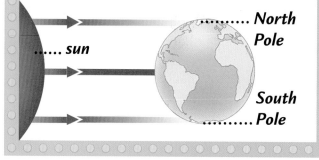

...... *sun*

.......... *North Pole*

*South Pole* ..........

### Arctic and Antarctic
The area around the North Pole is called the Arctic. Here, some animals live on the land and in the sea even during the freezing winters. The area around the South Pole is called the Antarctic. Here, most animals live in the sea, out of the fierce, cold winds. Even in summer, it is still so cold that only a few animals live on the land.

▶ Emperor penguins spend all their lives on and around the ice of the Antarctic.

◀ People such as the Inuit live in the Arctic. These Inuit children are wearing animal skins to keep themselves warm.

## Quiz Corner

● On a globe, where are the North and South Poles?

● Where do the Inuit live?

● Where do most of the animals of the Antarctic live?

Look at: North Pole, page 8; South Pole, page 12

# Polar Ice

In the Arctic and Antarctic, there are many different kinds of ice. On the land, huge sheets of ice form. These are called **ice caps**. Rivers of ice are called **glaciers**. They start in the mountains and flow slowly across the land toward the sea. Floating ice that forms on the ocean is called **pack ice**.

▲ Seals often swim beneath pack ice. Under their skin, they have a thick layer of fat, called **blubber**, that keeps them warm.

### Icebergs

At the coasts, large chunks of ice break off from glaciers and ice caps. These chunks of ice float in the sea and are called icebergs. As icebergs drift into warmer water, they start to melt and break up. But even small icebergs may take more than three years to melt.

▲ Only a small part of an iceberg shows above the water. Ships have to take care not to crash into ice hidden under the water.

**Life beneath the ice**
Millions of tiny shrimplike creatures called **zooplankton** live in the icy seas. Zooplankton are eaten by animals such as fish, seals, seabirds, and even huge whales. Without zooplankton, all kinds of creatures would starve.

# Quiz Corner

● Name three kinds of polar ice.

● What keeps seals warm while they swim under the ice?

● Why do ships have to steer clear of icebergs?

Look at: Arctic Tundra, page 10; Arctic People, page 24

# North Pole

The North Pole is in the middle of the Arctic Ocean. In winter, a thick, white sheet of ice covers the ocean for hundreds of miles in every direction. Around the edge of the ocean there are flat lands where small plants, but no trees, grow. These lands are known as the **tundra**. Farther south, there are huge forests.

▼ Mapmakers draw a circle, called the Arctic Circle, around the top of the Earth. The North Pole is in the middle of it.

*Ice covers the middle of the Arctic Ocean.*

*Much of the land around the Arctic Ocean is tundra.*

*Arctic Circle*

North Pole

▼ In early summer, caribou start their journey from the forests near the Arctic Circle to feed on the wild plants farther north.

▼ Arctic **glaciers** flow slowly down mountainsides toward the ocean.

## People of the Arctic

For thousands of years, people have been living in the Arctic. They live in small towns on the land around the Arctic Ocean. During the Arctic winter, people may need to melt the ice and snow to make fresh water.

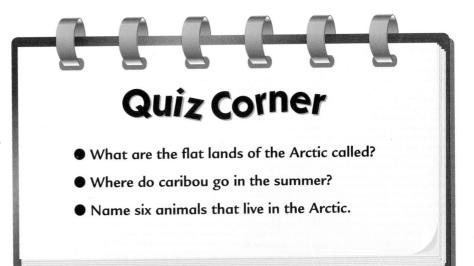

## Arctic wildlife

The different **habitats** of the Arctic are home to many animals and plants. Seals, whales, and otters swim in the icy waters and feed mostly on **zooplankton**. The tundra is home to small plants and many kinds of creatures. In the forest, wolves and bears hunt smaller animals, such as squirrels and birds.

## Quiz Corner

- What are the flat lands of the Arctic called?
- Where do caribou go in the summer?
- Name six animals that live in the Arctic.

# Arctic Tundra

In summer, snow on the Arctic **tundra** melts and the top layer of soil becomes soft. Leaves and flowers grow, berries ripen, and small insects, such as mosquitoes, hatch. Suddenly the air is full of the sound of buzzing insects, while the ground is a beautiful carpet of color.

▲ Musk oxen live on the tundra all year round. They protect themselves from hungry wolves by standing in a circle.

▲ The Arctic summer lasts from May to July. During this time, flowers such as this Arctic lupine brighten the tundra.

## Summer pools
The melted summer snow collects in the top layer of soil. Then pools and lakes start to form. The water cannot drain away because it is blocked by a layer of frozen ground called **permafrost**, which is deep under the soil.

### CHATTERBOX

The cold **temperatures** and lack of daylight make plants grow slowly. In the Arctic, it can take 100 years for a shrub to grow to 20 inches high. In a warm forest, trees can grow 100 times as high in the same amount of time!

10

## Summer visitors

In summer, caribou and other animals come to the tundra to feed on the plants. Thousands of birds also visit. Snow geese nest by the pools and eat grasses.

## Low-growing plants

Plants that flower in summer must also survive the winter. They grow close to the ground, so they do not get bent by the snow or wind. There are no trees there because their roots cannot grow through the permafrost.

## Quiz Corner

- How do musk oxen defend themselves from their enemies?

- Where do plants grow more slowly—in the Arctic or in a warm forest?

- Why don't trees grow on the tundra?

Look at: Penguins, page 18; Poles in Danger, page 28

# South Pole

The South Pole is in the middle of Antarctica, which is a huge **continent** almost twice the size of Australia. It is surrounded by the Antarctic Ocean. Small, slow-growing plants live along the rocky coastline, and thousands of seabirds **breed** there.

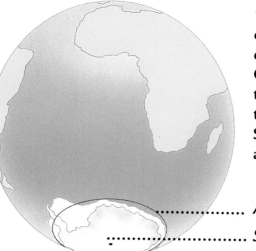

◀ Mapmakers draw a circle, called the Antarctic Circle, around the bottom of the Earth. The South Pole is at the center.

............... *Antarctic Circle*

............... *South Pole*

▲ Most of Antarctica, including many high mountains, is covered in thick ice. Only parts of the coastline are free from snow.

## The coldest continent

In the coldest parts of the Antarctic, water freezes as soon as it is poured into a glass. As the strong wind whips over the land, it cuts the ice into spectacular shapes. A few scientists live in the Antarctic in comfortable research stations. In summer, the scientists work outside. In winter, they work inside, sheltered from the wild storms and freezing **temperatures**.

## CHATTERBOX

The largest animal on Earth, the blue whale, lives in Antarctic waters. It grows up to 100 feet in length, which is as long as seven cars end to end.

## Life along the coast

Few plants or animals live in Antarctica. During summer, seals and penguins come to the coast to breed and give birth to their young. There, the babies are safe because there are few **predators**.

## Antarctic waters

It is slightly warmer in the water than it is on the land. Billions of tiny plants and animals called **plankton** live in the ocean. Many larger sea creatures feed on them.

▼ Colorful creatures live in the icy waters of the Antarctic Ocean.

*A sea urchin protects itself with long spines.*

*Coral is made of the skeletons of tiny animals.*

*If a starfish loses one of its arms, it grows a new one.*

*A sea anemone catches its food with its tentacles.*

*Sea spiders look like land spiders but can have between four and ten legs.*

*A sea slater has a hard shell to protect itself from other animals.*

## Quiz Corner

- What is the largest animal on Earth?
- Name two animals that come to the Antarctic coast to breed.
- How does a sea urchin protect itself?

Look at: Polar Birds, page 16; Penguins, page 18; Polar Bears, page 22

# Creatures of the Cold

Some creatures stay in the polar areas even in winter. Many polar animals have thick fur, feathers, or **blubber** to keep them warm. Foxes and hares live in the Arctic throughout the year, while penguins and albatross stay in the Antarctic all year round.

▼ This scene shows the beginning of an Arctic winter. These animals stay in the Arctic throughout the year.

## CHATTERBOX

People use the thick, soft feathers of the eider duck to make warm coats and bedding. But the eider duck had the idea first. The female plucks some of the feathers from her own breast to line her nest and keep her eggs warm.

*The Arctic fox starts to grow its white winter coat, so it will not be seen against the snow.*

*In summer, lemmings live above the ground. When winter arrives, they spend time under the snow, feeding on seeds in the soil.*

## Energy for the winter

During winter, polar animals have to survive for long periods with only a small amount of food. They stock up by eating as much as they can in summer—caribou eat all day and night. The extra food is stored as fat on their bodies, which, during winter, keeps them warm and gives them **energy**.

*A snowy owl hunts small animals such as lemmings.* .............

## Quiz Corner

- Name five animals that live in the Arctic all through winter.
- Where do lemmings find food in winter?
- How do Arctic squirrels spend winter?

## Winter naps

In winter, to save energy, polar animals do as little as possible. The polar bear spends most of the winter in its den, sleeping for many hours at a time. The Arctic squirrel also sleeps a lot, curling up in a snug burrow.

*Arctic hares find areas where the snow is thin so that they can dig for food.*

*The Arctic stoat is called an ermine once it has grown its white winter coat.*

15

Look at: Penguins, page 18

# Polar Birds

There are huge numbers of birds in the Arctic and Antarctic, but few stay all year. Most arrive in early summer, then fly to warmer countries at the start of autumn. Only a few types of birds, such as gulls and terns, are found in both the Arctic and the Antarctic.

▲ The albatross uses its long, narrow wings to help it glide and swoop over the stormy Antarctic Ocean.

## Antarctic birds
The albatross, one of the largest seabirds, lives around the Antarctic. It flies over the sea, dropping down to the surface to catch fish. Penguins are the best-known Antarctic birds. More than one million penguins live on the Antarctic coast.

▲ The ptarmigan has feathers on its legs and feet to keep them warm in the snow.

## Arctic birds
Many birds, such as puffins and geese, come to the Arctic in the summer to **breed** and raise their young. Ptarmigans live on the Arctic **tundra** all year round. The ptarmigan's summer feathers are the color of the rocks, and its winter feathers are white.

**CHATTERBOX**

Each year, Arctic terns spend the summer raising their young in the Arctic. Then they fly across the world to enjoy the Antarctic summer, which lasts from November to January. At the end of January, they fly back to the Arctic.

16

▼ Puffins nest in large groups along the rocky coasts of the Arctic. They feed on fish and are expert swimmers and divers.

## Quiz Corner

- When do most polar birds arrive at the poles?

- Name three Arctic birds.

- What are the best-known birds of the Antarctic?

- What do puffins and albatross feed on?

# Penguins

Many kinds of penguins live in the Antarctic. The biggest is the emperor penguin, which is about three feet tall. Penguins are unusual birds: they cannot fly but are excellent swimmers. They come on land only to lay their eggs and care for their chicks.

## CHATTERBOX

When penguins want to travel fast on snow or ice, they flop on to their stomachs and toboggan, pushing themselves along with their feet and wings.

▲ Emperor penguin parents take turns caring for their chick.

## Baby-sitting

In May, the female emperor penguin lays an egg. Then she goes out to sea to build up a supply of food, while the male stays with the egg, keeping it warm. In July, the mother returns with fish for the newly hatched chick.

▲ Adélie penguins feed on squid, fish, and **plankton**.

18

When Adélie penguins are on land, they stay together in large groups. When they are in the sea, they hunt separately.

## New feathers

When a penguin chick first hatches, it is covered in a coat of soft gray or brown feathers called down. After a few weeks, the chick begins to grow its shiny adult feathers.

## Super swimmers

The penguin's short legs and webbed feet are perfect for swimming, and its paddle-shaped wings work well as flippers. In summer, penguins molt, which means they lose all of their feathers. They wait for a new coat of waterproof feathers to grow before they go in the water again.

## Quiz Corner

- Can penguins fly?
- Does the mother or father emperor penguin look after the egg?
- What do Adélie penguins eat?
- What color are the feathers of a newly hatched penguin chick?

19

Look at: Polar Ice, page 6; Polar Bears, page 22

# Seals and Walruses

Seals live in both polar oceans, where they **breed** and feed along the coasts. The walrus comes from the same family of animals as the seal but lives only in the Arctic. Seals and walruses are **mammals**. The female gives birth to a baby, or pup, and feeds it with her milk.

### In and out of water

Seals spend a lot of time swimming. They can stay under water for up to one hour, but then they need to come to the surface to breathe. When the sea is frozen, they make breathing holes in the ice, called blow holes. Seals enjoy soaking up sunshine. They move in quick leaps onto the ice, then lie in the sun to warm themselves.

## CHATTERBOX

Seals can sleep under water. When they need to breathe, they rise to the surface. Then they sink back down again and continue sleeping.

▲ Many seal pups can swim in the sea and move on land almost as soon as they are born.

◀ Walruses huddle together to stay warm and to protect themselves from polar bears.

## Quiz Corner

● Where do walruses live?

● How do mother seals feed their babies?

● What are baby seals called?

● How do walruses keep warm?

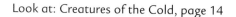

# Polar Bears

The polar bear lives in the Arctic and is one of the world's largest animals. It is twice the size of a lion. The polar bear has a layer of thick, soft fur next to its skin, then an outer coat of long hairs. When the polar bear swims, the long hairs stick together, helping to keep out the cold.

## Walking on ice

The polar bear has large, padded feet. Stiff hairs between the pads help the bear to grip, so it can walk and even run across slippery ice.

### CHATTERBOX

In winter, when the sea is frozen over, polar bears catch seals by waiting for them to come up for air at their blow holes. One slap from a polar bear's paw is enough to kill the seal.

▲ Polar bears spend most of their time at sea, either floating on the ice or swimming in the water.

## Hunting for food

Polar bears hunt for seals and fish in the sea. They also explore the **tundra**, eating grass and berries. In winter, when there is less food, they sometimes wander into towns. This can be dangerous for the bears because they may harm themselves on garbage found in trash cans.

## Polar bear cubs

In December, a female polar bear digs a den in the snow or ice. There, she gives birth to one or two cubs, then feeds them with her milk. When the cubs are three months old, the mother bear lets them go outside for the first time. The cubs live with their mother for up to two years while they learn how to swim and hunt.

▼ The mother polar bear stays in the den with her cubs, living off the fat stored in her body. When she finally leaves, she is thin and in need of food.

## Quiz Corner

- Do polar bears live in the Arctic or the Antarctic?
- What do polar bears eat?
- Why do polar bears visit towns?
- How long does a polar bear cub stay with its mother?

Look at: Lands of Snow and Ice, page 4; North Pole, page 8; Poles in Danger, page 28

# Arctic People

In the Arctic, people called the Inuit live along the coasts of Greenland, Canada, and Alaska. The Saami live farther south, in Lapland. In the past, the Inuit lived by hunting, while the Saami raised herds of reindeer for their milk, meat, and fur. Today, many Inuit and Saami work in the fishing, forestry, oil, and gas industries.

### An Inuit igloo

The Inuit of Canada used to spend the winter in ice houses called igloos. They shaped slabs of ice into a dome, then filled the cracks with snow. Inside the igloo, the Inuit ate and slept on a platform of ice covered with furs. They lit and heated the igloo with seal-oil lamps.

window made from clear ice

air hole

entrance

platform

▲ Today, when the Inuit are on long hunting trips, they stay overnight in igloos.

◀ The Saami often wear traditional clothing to take tourists on sleigh rides across the snow.

## Staying warm

In the past, Arctic people dressed in clothes made from animal furs or wool. They lived in houses made of rock, grass, or ice, or in animal-skin tents. Today, most Arctic people wear modern clothes and live in houses made from bricks and wood.

▲ Many people use snowmobiles rather than sleds to travel across the icy land.

## New industries

In the past, when Arctic people needed food, they caught fish. When they needed wood, they cut down trees. Today, fishing and forestry have become large Arctic industries, involving thousands of Inuit and Saami. Those who work in the fishing industry catch and pack fish to send all over the world.

## Quiz Corner

● Which groups of people live in the Arctic?

● How do many people travel in the Arctic today?

● Name two important Arctic industries.

Look at: Poles in Danger, page 28

# Polar Exploration

Nearly 100 years ago, explorers first reached the Poles. Since then, there have been many more **expeditions**. Today, scientists from all over the world work together in research stations in the Arctic and Antarctic. By studying the land and ice, they learn about our planet and how to care for it in the future.

◀ Scientists test the soil to see if it has been harmed by **pollution**.

▲ The Amundsen-Scott base is an American research station in Antarctica. Its dome shape helps to keep the snow off.

**Science in action**
The weather all around the world is affected by the weather at the Poles. Scientists in polar research stations study the wind, land, and ice to learn about the Earth's weather. They try to find out how our weather may change in years to come.

## SEE FOR YOURSELF

See why explorers wear layers of clothing to keep heat from escaping. Ask an adult to fill two plastic jars with warm water. Wrap cotton wool around one jar and leave the other uncovered. Take the **temperature** of the water in each jar after ten minutes. Which jar gets cold quicker?

## Preparing to explore

Just moving around in cold polar temperatures takes up a lot of **energy**, so explorers need to eat well. To keep the weight of their packs down, they take dried food, then mix it with snow or ice before cooking it. Explorers' clothing is warm, but light enough for them to move around in easily.

▼ Modern equipment and a lightweight sled help the polar explorer travel alone or with a small group of huskies.

*The explorer wears goggles to cut out the glare of the sun on the snow.*

*Warm gloves and boots keep the explorer's fingers and toes from being harmed by the cold.*

*Sleds, piled high with equipment, run on sturdy skis.*

*Huskies are useful for guarding the camp from other animals. Today, many explorers use snowmobiles rather than huskies to pull their sleds.*

Look at: Polar Exploration, page 26

# Poles in Danger

Today, some industries in the Arctic have polluted the air and water and destroyed parts of the **tundra**. **Pollution** from other parts of the world also damages polar areas. Countries are now working together to protect the polar lands and seas.

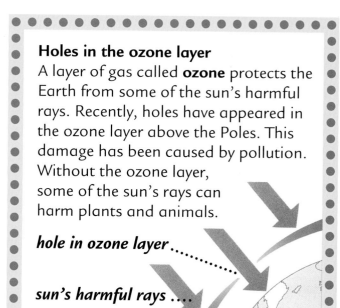

**Holes in the ozone layer**

A layer of gas called **ozone** protects the Earth from some of the sun's harmful rays. Recently, holes have appeared in the ozone layer above the Poles. This damage has been caused by pollution. Without the ozone layer, some of the sun's rays can harm plants and animals.

*hole in ozone layer* ..............

*sun's harmful rays* ....

▲ In parts of the Arctic, people have left litter on the land. These oil drums are a danger to wildlife.

**Arctic mining**

In the Arctic, people have mined for the coal, oil, and gas that lie under the ground. They have built pipelines and roads, taking land away from animals and plants.

▶ Underground oil pipes damage the **permafrost** and wildlife, so these pipes in Alaska were laid above ground.

28

▲ Whales have been hunted for their oils and meat for so long that they are difficult to find. They are now protected.

**Keeping the Poles clean**
In 1989, there was a large oil spill in the Arctic and millions of animals died. In the Antarctic, to avoid a similar accident, countries have agreed not to build any oil, gas, or coal mines. People would like to keep the Arctic and Antarctic among the cleanest and least polluted places on Earth.

# Quiz Corner

● How have some industries harmed the Arctic?

● Name an animal that is now protected from being hunted.

● Where are the holes in the ozone layer?

# Amazing Facts

● Less than 6 inches of rain or snow falls on Antarctica each year. This is the same yearly rainfall as in parts of the very dry Sahara Desert in Africa.

☆ *Emperor penguins dive deeper than any other polar birds. They can dive as deep as a quarter mile in search of food.*

● The Weddell seal in the Antarctic and the ringed seal in the Arctic spend entire winters under the ice. They come up to their blow holes for air, then go straight down in the water again.

☆ *The deepest layers of ice in the Antarctic are at least 200,000 years old. Many of the small plants there are more than 100 years old.*

● A team of 12 huskies can pull a sled that weighs up to half a ton—the weight of a small car.

☆ *In summer, patches of the Antarctic Ocean are so full of **zooplankton** that the surface of the water sometimes looks red.*

● The holes in polar fishing nets are big enough to let young fish slip back into the water. This allows the fish to grow old enough to **breed**, which keeps up the number of fish in the ocean.

☆ *The polar bear has such a strong sense of smell that it can smell seals through several yards of snow.*

● Icebreakers are strong ships that break through thick sheets of **pack ice**, making a path for other ships to use. Some icebreakers can break ice more than 10 feet thick.

☆ *The largest recorded iceberg was bigger than the entire island of Jamaica. It was 208 miles long and 60 miles wide.*

# Glossary

**blubber** The layer of fat that lies under the skin of some animals. It keeps them warm in winter and when they swim in icy water.

**breed** When animals mate to produce young of their kind.

**continent** A huge area of land. There are seven continents in the world.

**energy** What makes living things move and grow. Animals and plants receive energy from food or sunlight.

**expedition** A long journey made by explorers.

**glacier** A river of ice that moves slowly over land toward the sea.

**habitat** The place where a plant or animal grows or lives.

**ice cap** A sheet of ice covering part of the land in the Arctic or the Antarctic.

**mammals** Animals that give birth to live young and feed them with the mother's milk.

**ozone** A layer of gas around Earth that protects the planet from some of the sun's harmful rays.

**pack ice** A floating layer of frozen sea.

**permafrost** The thick layer of soil under the **tundra** that stays frozen even in the summer.

**plankton** Tiny plants and animals that live in the ocean. Animal plankton is called **zooplankton**.

**pollution** Dirt or garbage that can harm Earth and its plants and animals.

**predator** An animal that hunts and eats other animals.

**temperature** How hot or cold something is.

**tundra** The flat lands that surround the Arctic Ocean. The tundra is covered in snow in the winter but is home to many plants and animals all through the year.

**zooplankton** Animal **plankton**.

# Index

Published in the USA by
C.D. Stampley Enterprises, Inc.,
Charlotte, NC, USA.
Created by Two-Can Publishing Ltd.,
London. English-language edition
© Two-Can Publishing Ltd., 1997

Managing Editor: Robert Sved
Art Director: Carole Orbell
Editor: Janet De Saulles
Picture research: Laura Cartwright
Consultant: Dr Bernard Stonehouse
Artwork: Bill Donohoe, Teri Gower,
Mel Pickering and Peter Bull
Production: Adam Wilde
Additional Research: Inga Phipps

ISBN 1-58087-004-X

Photographic Credits: Front cover:
Bruce Coleman Ltd; pp. 4/5: Bruce
Coleman Ltd; p. 5(t): B&C Alexander;
p. 6(l), pp. 6/7(c): Oxford Scientific
Films; p. 8(b): Robert Harding;
pp. 8/9(c): Planet Earth Pictures;
p. 10: BBC Natural History Unit;
p. 12: Pictor International; p. 16,
p. 17: Planet Earth Pictures; p. 18:
Bruce Coleman Ltd; pp. 20/21(c):
Ardea Ltd; p. 21(t): B&C Alexander;
p. 22: BBC Natural History Unit;
p. 24: B&C Alexander; p. 25(tl):
Pictor International; p. 25(c), p. 26,
p. 28 (l&r): B&C Alexander; p. 29:
Ardea Ltd.